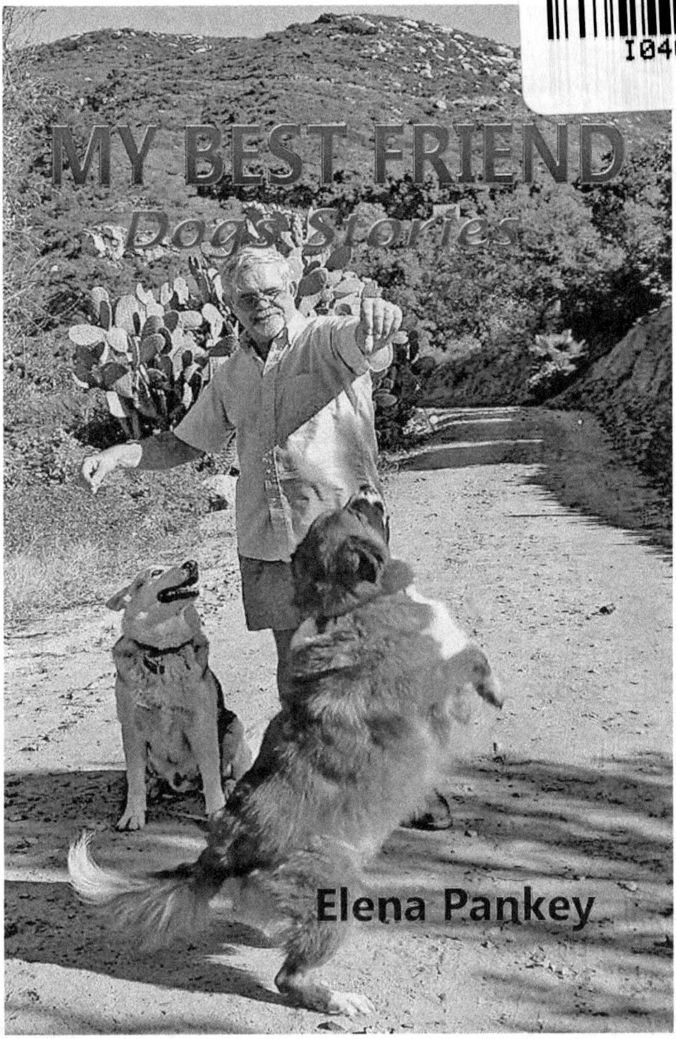

MY BEST FRIEND
Dogs Stories

Elena Pankey

MY BEST FRIEND
Dogs Stories

Elena Pankey

ISBN-13: 978-1-950311-38-5

AllRightsReserved@2019ElenaPankey

Contents

Leningrad	5
Effort	7
Dreams	8
Reasons	9
New Member	12
First Happy Days	14
Friendship	16
Family	19
Circumstances	21
New Life	24
Ranger	25
Alaskan Husky	27
Ranch Dog	29
Memory	34
Chow Chow	35
Zuynka	37
Tuzik and Sonia	38
German Shepherd	41
Interesting Facts	43
Scientists about Dogs	46
Love your dog	48
Today	53

Afterword	54
Our Favorite Pets	55
About Author	57
Copy Rights Page	58

Leningrad

From 1979 to 1995, I lived in the most beautiful city of Russia, Leningrad (St. Petersburg). It was a very interesting and difficult time. For 300 years, Leningrad was a living monument to Russia's past. Peter the Great founded it, but Catherine the Great established most of the beautiful architectural ensembles. In 1991, Leningrad officially became St. Petersburg once again. People reclaimed the original name of the city. Once again, the city had become "the Russian door to Europe," and the center of the 300-year debate about Russia's relationship to itself, to modernity, and to the West.

The most difficult question of Russian life in that period, as always, was where to live or how to get an apartment. However, I moved  to the cultural center of Russia - Leningrad - from a small resort town on the Black Sea, Gelendzik. I had precisely one goal: to stay there and become successful. I was ambitious, beautiful, and elegant, with good taste; and never had a problem meeting men.

Once in Hermitage I met Valery Bulat, who was from Ukraine. Valery was a very kind, ingenuous and handsome young man. He was a student of an art college, loved to draw, and spent all his time at home doing it. It looked like he was a very talented person, and I tried to get him established in the new city. The most important thing for me was that he paid a lot of attention and helped me with my eight years old daughter. Therefore, soon we got married. After our marriage, he dropped out of his college and moved into my apartment. I hoped it would be a happy and lasting relationship.

During 1982-1987, I was a student at the prestigious Leningrad State University and went there for the evening lectures. Sometimes I took Valery with me to enjoy the intellectual life we had there. For my diploma, I asked Valery to make several wonderful illustrations.

At that time, we lived very modesty and often did not have enough food. I had a very small income, even though I was working at several jobs. Valery did not work in the 1980s. First, his explanation was that he needs to be in a collage, and then he just could not find a job.

However, many years later, Valery wrote, "I remember our life in Leningrad and the University. How we all were passionate about symbolism." The lectures in Leningrad State University, the world known Hermitage, and meeting with intelligent people had a big influence on us both. Our world viewpoint, philosophy, the formation of the artistic personality was forming in those years of 1980-1990s and this determined our fate.

Effort

I am a very enthusiastic person and was sure that humor and laughing are especially helpful for the happiness of family. In addition, laughter  is a good instrument of love, and the most important thing in a married life. I always thought that if I can laugh with my partner over my mistakes, or on his mistakes, we would overcome any discontent or misunderstanding in any relationship. Laughing, we will show each other that we are both imperfect and each of us have many sides for improvement.

We seemed to live very joyfully with Valery and despite all difficulties, raised my daughter and were happy. On the other hand, we did not have our own children. When we visited Valery's parents in Ukraine, I saw that his mother enjoyed sewing and knitting babies' dresses for other married members of the family. In the hectic days of my life, I forgot that some time ago during my previous sad marriage, I got the best medical contraceptive, inserted in the cervix. I was reminded about it much later and already after I separated from Valery. It was one of many anecdotes of my Russian life. The memory of this incident later inspired me after "perestroika" to open my own medical business.

Dreams

Soon after our marriage, Valery and I got a kitten and called him Tosha. We trained him to use our toilet, and Tosha created a special ritual  for it. He told us about it in advance, saying "meow." Then he opened the toilet door with his paw, jumped up onto the seat and did all that was necessary there, standing on its edge. However, if we did not wash it off immediately, he was very angry and rushed around like a mad man.

We pampered our pet in every possible way, indulging his whims, letting him jump everywhere and do whatever he likes. Over time, Tosha became accustomed to our love and permissiveness. As a result, he was spoiled and overconfident.

In all ways, our cat mostly loved and respected his owner Valery. As a sign of his deep devotion, Tosha slept on the bed with Valery, spending nights lying down at Valery's feet or near his head. During the day, while Valery was drawing, Tosha enjoyed sitting next to him smelling his paintings. Sometimes Tosha was trying to make Valery happier, and jumped on his easel to mix the paint. Usually, after that we saw his paw-prints everywhere. Tosha also constantly fallowed Valery everywhere in the apartment.

 And in return, Valery found consolation and comfort in his cat, but still was yearning for a child.

Our smart cat Tosha was generously giving us the feeling of his need in reliability, warmth and cosines. Sometimes our cat looked at all of us with his mystical eyes as if to say: "Strive to the moon. Then you are most likely to be among the Stars." This was our slogan for a long time, and maybe because of that, all our dreams come true.

***

Reasons

Every summer we visited my grandmother who lived in the small resort Gelendzik, on the Black Sea where I grew up. My grandmother Anna was a very hospitable and kind woman. This time we came to her with my new husband, our cat Tosha and dog named Brake. Even though she was very surprised to see our big company, she warmly and very cordially accepted us all, as always.

When a warm and pleasant evening came, we took Tosha out into the yard. He rummaged a little bit a hole there in the dirt, then looked at us and ran away to the neighbors. We regret that we did not tie our cat to the leg of the bed and did not keep him at home, but it was too late. So that vacation Tosha spent in a fierce battle with local bacchanals for territorial dominance

Our much wiser, but still not broken, romantic Tosha spent the remaining days of our vacation high on the roof of the house. Tosha had a comfortable position there to see all around and was covered by the apricot tree from all extraneous eyes. He was lying quietly in the sun, licking his battle wounds, and thinking that it would be much safer and more pleasant to observe someone else's secular life from afar. As a touring outsider, he was not accepted into the public life of the local revelers. Yes, he no longer aspired to this paradise, where nobody was even fed free, as he had been all his life.

The resort life brought Tosha only disappointment and seemed meaningless. During his turbulent epic, Tosha reconsidered his own comfortable past life in St. Petersburg. Now he believed in the value of what he had before, and began to cherish it even more. But he still dreamed to have a big, strong and good friend, who would protect him in his next time on the Black Sea.

At the end of August, we returned to St. Petersburg, where it was already quite cool. There were endless rains and blowing winds. On the eve of winter, we did not open more windows on the balcony. Therefore, our Tosha no longer walked along the cornice, but just sat at the glassed-in window and looked at the gray sky where the birds seldom appeared. The time of his favorite hunt was over, and he again felt lonely or bored. In the evening, when we were returning from work, he jumped on the shoulders of his beloved owner, rubbing against his ear and whispering something plaintive to him.

During the day, he often was sitting next to Valery's easel while he was drawing. Tosha continued to talk to him about different mysterious things. It was clear that often he mostly complained about my or Lila's faults or that we did not give him enough attention. He recollected that we refused to eat his fresh sparrows he was bringing to my bed, and that we did not appreciate his hunting on the balcony. Then, he mentioned that we did not serve on time his favorite fish. Most importantly, he remembered that he was subjected to severe tests in our resent journey to the resort town, where the local bully cats attacked him. Evidently, it turned out that Tosh felt himself an unrecognized genius, and we neglected to distinguish all his talents.

As a result, from the endless Tosha mewing and purring, we realized that he clearly expressed the desire to take care of someone. He did not find self-satisfaction in those around him, or in loving his family, because we spent the greater part of the day outside the home, at work or at school. He wanted to have a constant and devoted friend, with whom he would share his fish and spend the whole day together. He needed a true and loving comrade who would respect and appreciate him. Tosha looked more and more unhappy and again became depressed. It was the time to help him. We found the original way and bought him a German shepherd puppy. There was a new and happier page of Tosha's life.

New Member

People's attitude towards living beings determines the quality of their soul and character. Sometimes people do not think that their pets have  feelings and simple thoughts, and their inner meaning is to make us happy. When we have pets at home, our loyal friends follow our every step and their goal is to please us.

We finally came to the conclusion that we had several good reasons to get a dog. Obviously, dogs are always more than just cuddly companions. The pets bring real health benefits to their owners. For example, studies have found that dog owners have lower blood pressure and lower cholesterol than non-dog owners do. Having a dog around can lead to lower levels of stress for both adults and kids, and to decrease the risk of asthma in children.

Caring for a dog can help children grow up more secure and active or provide valuable companionship for older adults. Moreover, dog owners generally have a stronger immune system, helping them to stay well and spend less time getting over sickness. We also read that a dog can be a comfort to people who crave unconditional interaction with another living being.  Dogs can decrease levels of human loneliness and give humans a sense of purpose as they care for their animal companions. Living with a dog brings longevity and reduced risk for heart disease.

This is why people say, "a dog is a man's best friend." Dogs are silent obedient companions, who always listen and love their masters unconditionally, without arguments or discussion, no matter what. They take on themselves many emotional burdens of their masters. Maybe this is why dogs live such a short life?

Our dog story began when Valery and I had been married about three years. Since I was the one who was providing for the family, I was working a lot, while trying to finish University. At the same time my husband wanted to have a child, my daughter dreamed about a workmate, and our cat Tosha asked for a friend. Therefore, I felt that I had to do something very quickly to save our marriage. Finally, I decided to make everybody busy with thoughts that are more new, duties and responsibilities. One day I agreed to buy a puppy, but with one condition. The dog should be taken to a special training school to be a home guard for our apartment, even though we were not in a big apartment, with tiny space for a rapidly growing family. But Russians have a saying: better to live happily in a crowded room than unhappily in a palace. Anyway, when a puppy appeared in our home everybody was happy, including our neat and tidy cat.

First Happy Days

The puppy came to us straight from Germany. My husband and daughter went to meet him at the station. In addition, Tosha and I were waiting for them in our warm and cozy home. The puppy was amazing, very thoroughbred, with a very long and clean pedigree. And he looked like a very clever, all-silently understanding dog. All his documents were in excellent condition. His name came with him and it was written in his passport: "Brake". We were all extremely happy about the new member of the family and were not concerned about this strange English name.

For the first several weeks, Tosha also was very happy and even inspired by a sudden change in the rhythm of his life. He was not even jealous that all our attention went to the fat and awkward puppy. The generous and matured Tosha forgave all the turmoil that our new cute guy has created for us all. In addition, that beautiful puppy was funny and also very kind. He was extremely happy to meet everyone and liked everything around him, but he was constantly hungry and was very fond of eating, especially some fish.

But soon Tosh noticed that our dog creates too much new work for him. In the first days of arrival, the puppy Brake made all his "necessities" everywhere and anywhere in the apartment. We just did not have time to run to the street with him from the fourth floor. So, where this "need" caught the puppy, there he did it. And Tosha was going after the puppy and tried to clean everything up or dig it all and cover it somehow. But nothing was disappearing anywhere.

Our cat had an obsession about cleanliness, and he got sick from the fact that he did not have time to clean up the dog. After several days of such a struggle for purity, Tosha was exhausted and defeated. He could not even stand fatigued. Finally, Tosha stopped his ardent desire to teach the dog to go to the same "human" cultural toilet, as he did. Tosha just stopped moving on the floor, it was above his dignity. He just jumped from the cupboard to the closet.

However, to an even greater concern of our cat, the dog was constantly hungry. We fed them both at the same time. Our pampered cat loved to eat slowly, with the understanding of this pleasure, carefully experiencing his food and enjoying every sip. He always eagerly was waiting the hour of feeding. This procedure took him long and pleasant minutes.

Brake very quickly just swallowed everything that was put on his plate. And then dog carefully cleaned his plate, looked at the cat and whispered, that food to his growing organism is now more important than a lazy cat. And then he immediately stuck his face in a bowl in the bowl and tried to eat what was left there. However, Tosha, taught by a gang of local cats in the southern resort, knew how to stand up for his fighting skills. He immediately grabbed the dog in the nose. And when I shouted at him, Tosha explained that it was just a little warning to an expensive but ungrateful family member. The unsuspecting Brake was simply stunned by such a rebuff and never touched the cat's food again.

Friendship

Soon after that, Tosha started a new hobby and followed it for a long time. Trying to show Brake that cleanliness in the house is his main priority, after dinner Tosha tried to clean the huge dog's face with his little tongue. First of all, he tightly clung to the dog's neck so that he did not run away and began to lick it, trying to make the dog perfectly clean. However, he did not have enough saliva, and he quickly got tired. In addition, I had to wash myself. All these new worries and problems really upset Tosh. Therefore, since he was not able to handle that incredibly time-consuming task, Tosha slightly bit the snout of the dog, at the same time whipping him with his paw, as if to teach himself.

Brake was a very kind and patient dog. He thought it was some kind of special game or the traditions of his new home. He suffered all the cat is wasting with great patience and inevitability. Although the size of our sheepdog increased every day, Brake was still quite a small puppy. Arriving to us, he naturally took the cat for the supreme leader, besides the wise resorts.

Winter came with its frosts and snowstorm. To go out with, Brake had his master - Valery, who was freer than I was. Usually early in the morning Valery would take Break on his favorite walk. But if my husband was not at home, then I had to walk the dog. If the shepherd suddenly saw his beloved master, then his joy was without limit. If I, not keeping a strong dog, fell on a slippery sidewalk, he continued to drag me a few meters in the snow, until he reached Valery. Then he jumped on his chest and happily licked it.

Our dog loved his walks in the wasteland, where other comrades appeared in muzzles and leashes. He was jogging about the snowdrifts and mud with a loud barking. In addition, when they returned, Brake was accustomed to jump into the bath immediately to wash his paws. The bathroom was covered from the top to the bottom with dirt, Brake shook furiously, pouring all and all the remaining drops, and rushed to watch what they gave to eat.

After eating dog went to his place under the table, and Valery cleaned the bath tub from the black mud of his beloved dog.

Although Tosha was very tiny compared to the dog, but he was older and wiser than a puppy. In general, life under one roof for all sentient beings should be as pleasant and comfortable as possible. That is why Tosh felt the need to make friends with the dog.

They gradually became really good friends, sharing everything with each other, including their masters. When the dog returned from a street walk, Tosha joyfully ran to him to find out what he brought with him, in addition to fleas. What other news was out there in the dangerous and so difficult world of adventures and fears? Brake carefully took the cat's small head into its huge mouth and gently licked it, playing. The lessons that our cat gave on the quest for cleanliness did not pass in vain. But still Tosh felt the superiority of his race. He walked around the apartment with his tail lifted, he jumped where he wanted, and at any moment, he was kindly treated by Valery and therefore considered Brake his pet.

In winter, the apartment was quite cold. Most often Tosha slept between our bed and a little warm portable heater. Sometimes at night, he

moved closer to us and lay down on the feet of my husband. And over time, he began to move very close to Valera's head, loudly purring him the night lullabies. Valera was not bothered. Cat was creating additional warmth and comfort.

In addition, during the winter Tosha spent time on the back of the dog, getting warm up. It looked like a happy time for them both. However, sometimes the cat wanted to emphasize once again who exactly was the master of the house and lay down on this special dog place. Brake approached his mat, saw impudent Tosha sweetly there asleep, and in his heart he had no strength to disturb the cat. He was modestly laid to his side, and somehow fiddling with a small rag that served as a dog's place.

The cat always felt his privileged position and enjoyed it. The good-natured dog easily conceded everything to him and recognized his authority. Brake sometimes had a hard time, but he understood that for a happy life in a small apartment, peace was needed. So the cat and the dog were friends, despite their incredibly contradictory characters. By their peaceful life, they refuted the proverb about the warring sides of the two beings. And the old saying "to live like a cat and a dog" was not at all glaring truthfulness.

Family

One day, just before the trip south, Brake got sick with a plague, although he had all the vaccinations done on time. We did not expect this and were very worried.  Trying to save the clever dog and cure this serious illness, we ourselves injected him every four hours. My daughter was boiling syringes in the kitchen, then I was holding the dog, and she was sticking medicine to him. This treatment was a long one, and we could not postpone the long-awaited trip to rest.

On the train, Valery spent days and nights in the vestibule with Brake, continuing to give him the necessary injections. Adoration of the dog to Valera was his strongest feeling and he obediently endured everything that he did.

Arriving again to visit my grandmother Anna, now with a cat and a dog, we settled again in the same room, in a small room with a terrace. Although in those years in the shops of the resort Gelendzhik were empty, there was enough fish on the Black Sea coast for everyone. And this time we cooked Mojva and Hake, but already to all members of the family. A couple of times, our cat still ventured to flee on the night date. However, at home he was waiting for a strict Brake, who slightly scolded the cat, reminding him of the danger of walking alone. Finally, Tosha decided to tell Brake about the local mafia and after that, his walks alone stopped. Brake loudly barked to the entire district, and now instead of night cat shows, we could not fall asleep from the eventual skirmishes.

Back in St. Petersburg, I decided that our dog should fulfill his mission to serve and at least guard our apartment. Therefore, for this very special preparation, it was decided to send Lila and Valera to the dog breeding club. After graduating with honors from all classes, he got many first prizes at all contests for which we took him.

After several months of training, his dog's breast glistened and sparkled with all-fire awards and medals. But although our Brake was very talented, he was too kind for a service sheepdog. He had an awesome appearance like all shepherds, but in fact, we could not teach him how to be aggressive. So our dreams of a dog protecting and guarding our apartment were not destined to come true. However, we loved our pets. Brake was really like a child for my husband, and was an equal member of our family. My goal, to take care of everyone and make all happy, was crowned with success.

Circumstances

In the early 1990s, Russia started its extraordinary transformations ("perestroka"). It changed from a communist dictatorship into a multiparty democracy. But some described Russia's economic performance in the 1990s as a "tragedy of historic proportions". Following a failed putsch by communist hardliners, Yeltsin agreed with the leaders of Ukraine and Belarus to dissolve the Soviet Union, leaving Russia independent.

At that time, many lost themselves in the new conditions of the "perestroika" that had begun, did not know how to live and perceived social changes tragically.

At the same time, I had lost all my jobs as a guide in the museums. Nevertheless, I had many good connections, and my friends one day invited me to join their new pharmaceutical business. I took it very seriously and put into it all the money I had and all of my attention. I also turned

"like a squirrel in a wheel," to live well and allow myself a lot. Soon I became very successful. After one year of my active work at my own business, I bought a new car and another apartment for my daughter Lila.

In the 1990s Valery attended restoration workshops in Leningrad, worked a little, felt that he must have freedom and not real job. He also often traveled alone to Odessa or to his hometown in Ukraine.

However, I trusted him and was sure, that all those six years we have lived in harmony. However, gradually my fatigue accumulated, and I more and more felt the burden of the hard work and necessity to support alone our family. I tired of working constantly in several places and providing my husband with the conditions for creativity, which did not bring any income.

Finally, my patience was broken and I again started to convince Valery that he needed at least a little formal work for money. Then, I went  to the director of the school where my daughter was a student and begged her to give a job for Valera as a teacher of drawing. To my surprise, she agreed, even though Valery did not have good education to be a teacher.

The school was in the courtyard of our house, and everyone was very close and comfortable. However, after half a year, I noticed that Valera comes home later and later. Then Lila finally told me, embarrassed and crying that he remains in a closed classroom with her young English teacher. As we soon learned, Valery had a short affair with this woman. I did not want to forgive and we divorced. Our happy world, which seemed to be forever, collapsed suddenly and without turning. I could not forgive such treacherous betrayal, and after the divorce, I drove Valera out of our apartment forever.

At the same time, I continued to work a lot as a tour guide and often was traveling with tourists out of town. To my sorrowful regret, I could not keep our animals at home. Therefore, our loving cat Tosha and devoted friend Brake left with my ex-husband. For a while, Valera rented a room from a friend. I did not know the address where Brake was living and could not visit him to console. We never saw our beloved animals again. Our wonderful dog Brake did not live long. Valera often left him alone at the friend's house. I did not know the address and could not visit him. Brake very much yearned for all family members. Soon Valera moved forever to his mother, to his homeland, to Ukraine, and took Tosha with him. However, our dog Brake could not handle the enduring separation; he died soon from the anguish of a broken heart.

New Life

In the middle of 1990s, St. Petersburg began experiencing the peak of banditry. To escape the persecution of the mafia, I tried hiding from the gangster's racketeering, and moved to California.

Once I was surprised to meet one very smart American student in the class where I studied English. He wrote his impression about Russia of 1990s: "If you want to celebrate liberation, it is the liberation of the great Russian people that deserved celebrating. Historians one day will cite the failure of the U.S. government to form a strong partnership with Russia as one of the greatest strategic blunders of all time. Instead of welcoming Russia to the West, the U.S. government treated it like a Third World country. However, I expect great things from Russia. I expect it will rise Phoenix-like from the ashes of communism, and one-day lead the world in many areas. I look forward to hearing the music and reading the literature that a new, reborn Russia will surely produce."

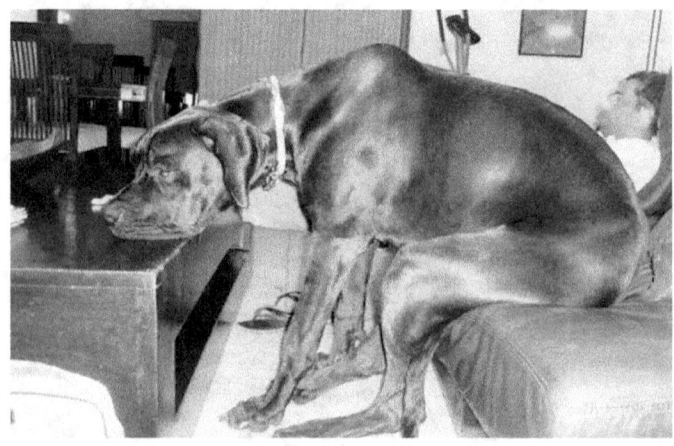

Ranger

In August 1999, we were renting a house in a little Californian village Bonsall. One day we visited my Russian friend Irina at her job. There her co-workers kept a young dog Eskimo Husky named Ranger. They found him lying on a Highway with bleeding feet. It looked like, soon after a big California fire, he tried to find his Master and ran for a long time.

Since he had a nametag, they called the number many times, hoping to find his owner, but nobody answered. Therefore, Ranger lived in Irina's work place where she was the only woman. He became accustomed to ride in a man's car and liked it very much. He probably thought that riding is his main purpose and job in his life.

Once Irina asked if we would take Ranger to our house and adopt him. We did not think long and decided to go to her and get him. He met us.

When we saw the dog, we were amazed at its beauty and nobility or status. Ranger was about 2 years old, handsome, trustful, open and kind. He desperately needed a house, a master or just somebody to love.

He remembered that he already had once his home and loving family. He had white-gray wool and had blue eyes. This especially struck us. We have not seen dogs with blue eyes before. Ranger stretched out and became alert. He looked at us with some hope and at the same time with apprehension.

At this time one of the workers came. Ranger rushed to his chest and licked him with devotion and joy. It was evident that the dog loves this man very much. The man took the dog to us in the car and we left. All the way, Ranger was looking out the window, rushing around the backseat of our huge Chevrolet, and whined. He was only two years old, but he had already suffered two irreparable losses of his first beloved masters.

We prepared for him a huge booth, bedding and everything necessary for comfort. When we arrived at our rented house, we placed Ranger on the patio, tying him to an umbrella. We gave him food and water. However, he did not eat. He longed for those who sheltered him before us. He tossed on a leash and tried to jump over the patio railing. Out of anguish and despair, he scattered food and spilled water. His rope was not long and he hung on it trying to escape through the fence.

We took him inside the house. However, even there he did not get peace and wanted to run away. It was very difficult to take him for a walk. He was very strong, and always tried to go somewhere just to the side.

But the time has passed. Ranger's hope to find one of his former owners was almost gone. And then we moved to the ranch.

Alaskan Husky

A working sled dog, the typical Alaskan Husky is a blend of various Nordic breeds, depending on the breeder's preferences and needs in a sled dog. Pulling ability and team player qualities are more important than  looks. Alaskan Huskies are not typically sold as pets but are sometimes found through rescue groups and can make good companions if their exercise needs are met.

The Alaskan Husky is more often seen as a working or competitive dog than solely as a family companion. He is an active dog and is best suited to a home where he has an opportunity to run on a daily basis. An athletic owner who can fulfill his strong desire to run and pull will make this dog happy, but one who leaves the dog in the home or backyard with nothing to do will come home to a scene of epic destruction.

Alaskan Huskies are great companions for hikers and backpackers and of course are naturals at such dog sports as sledding and skijoring. You will also see them performing well in agility, herding, obedience and rally.

With his heritage as a hard-working sled dog, the Alaskan Husky is intelligent and easy to train with positive reinforcement techniques such as praise, play and food rewards. That said he likes to do things his own way. Be firm, and keep training interesting.

The Alaskan Husky is an escape artist and can be a digger. Confine him to a yard with a fence that cannot be dug under or jumped over. An underground electronic fence will not stop an Alaskan Husky if he really wants to leave the yard.

The people-loving Alaskan Husky needs to live in the house with his family. It is an unhappy Alaskan Husky who is relegated to the backyard with little or no human companionship. If you do so, his barking and howling will be the least of your concerns.

The Alaskan Husky is a type rather than an actual breed. There is no breed standard for him; each breeder selects for the qualities that are most important to him or her. Different types of Alaskan Huskies do different jobs. Freighting dogs pull heavy loads. Sprinters go fast for short distances. Other dogs have the stamina to go long distances.

Ranch Dog

First, we kept Ranger around the house on a chain, from which he always tried to break.

Everyone needs kind words that would inspire. A faithful dog holds kind words especially dear. This Shepherd is a very smart dog and seems he understands any word. Soon Ranger realized that the main person at the ranch was my husband, and he decided to love and obey only Victor. Ranger was always waiting for the Master near Vic's office door. Although Victor was a kind man, he spoke little. However, Ranger was always waiting for him near the office door and the intelligent dog understood every word. His favorite activity was still a truck ride. When he saw through the crack that my husband was about to leave, he immediately jumped up and ran after him. Then he jumped into the truck and thought that it was his job. He needed to feel his need for people, he wanted to be useful.

We traveled a lot at that time. And soon my daughter Lala came to me and was engaged in her own little daughter. They needed to adapt to new living conditions and to social change. All were busy with their own problems and concerns. No one had enough time or energy for others, much less for a dog. So, Ranger was left to himself.

Everybody needs some rewords for their job, devotion and loyalty. So our dog watched for a while a lot of squirrels and rabbits around our hills. Then he figured that there is too much fresh food running here without any use! So from time to time, he gets a rabbit for his dinner. As he secretly explained, "he tired from our "Scientific" dry food every day and badly needed something refreshing".

His constant desire, chief instinct, was the desire to run and run. In addition, we, without knowing anything about the features of this breed of dogs, and not having fences, kept him on a long chain. Our short walks did not give him proper relief, and he was very unhappy.

Several times, he still broke and ran very far. Ranger always ran along the highway that passed close to our hill, and ran until it got tired.

Then someone found him. Since this breed of dogs needs human communication and loves people, it could be easily called up and take along with any child who was kind to him. But people just called us. I had to go after him and take the dog, shaking from suspense.

Alaskan husky, who loves people, would have to live in a house with his family. He became especially miserable in the backyard, without human intercourse. We did not even know that, and his nighttime howl did not let us sleep.

**

Unhappy Fate pursued Ranger. One day Vic was driving his tractor and moved mulch around the closest hill. Ranger lied down on the front yard. Another truck stood nearby. I came and asked Victor if he needs more room for his job and maybe I would move this truck from his way. He nodded and I walked to take Ranger from the front yard to his place. Victor misunderstood me, jumped in this truck, and moved back very fast. I tried to warn Vic about the Ranger on the road, but my husband had earplugs and could not hear me well. Ranger found himself under the wheels. I cried, our dog cried and we all were scared. However, this time our dog was lucky.

**

Since we live on the ranch, we have some special problems regarding the ranch life. One of them is coyotes and wild dogs. Almost every night a lot of coyotes come very close to our house and make a lot of noise!

They bark, yell and cry so loud that it keeps us awake.

Since we lived on the ranch, we had special problems with the life of the ranch. One of them was jackals and wild dogs. Almost every night a lot of jackals came very close to our home. They howled and barked, trying to frighten someone, screaming while hunting for hares and constantly bothering everyone. But they did not dare to attack the huge, but tied dog.

In addition, the courageous and inexperienced Ranger circled around his pillar, not hiding in the booth that stood nearby. Besides, he did not have the habit of barking. He just howled like a wolf from longing and sadness. Then his rope was wound around the tree to which he was tied. Nearby were bushes and he became very confused, could not move, and barely breathed.

Ranger especially liked digging holes. Maybe from inactivity and in the absence of any occupation, he endlessly dug something and dug around him. Pitying the dog, we tried to install an underground electronic fence. But this did not stop the Alaskan Husky. He still ran again and again.

Several times even wild dogs came to our hill with Ranger and engaged him in battle. Fighting a pack of dogs was hard, especially on a leash. And Ranger beat silently. Finally, we heard him screaming in pain and came out of the gun. They ran away from our shots, but not far. Then they also settled down in a pack on the top of a hill that was opposite the house, and they waited until we left. They were eager to take his food and finish the courageous, but one dog. This time, feral, hungry dogs tortured him badly, and we had to take him to the doctor to sew up wounds.

Probably we really would not pay very close attention to them but one day a tragedy happened to our wonderful dog. In the morning, April 15, at 7 am. Victor came to me and said : " Ranger needs our help, he was terribly injured." I came out of the house and saw bleeding Ranger near the porch. He obviously had strong pain, suffered from many wounds and looked pitiful and torn apart. Around the front yard, there were several blood spots.

Victor usually drives and checks his employees in the morning.  Ranger used to go with him and thought that this is his real job. Ranger is very responsible and took it very seriously. Despite his horrible wounds he moved to the sound of Victor's truck with strong intention to go to work even thought, he was in bad condition and almost could not move. It was very touching. I put him on the rug and started to clean his wound. There were 50 of them! Wild dogs horribly bit him! He could not get rid of them because he was tied up and winding around the Christmas tree. When the wild pack came and started to tear him, he could not go away. He just moved around the Christmas tree until his collar was so tight up that he could not move at all. The bite him and bite. He was too trustful, too open, too kind. He did not expect them - his former "friends" who eat his food and drank his water almost every night, - to be so cruel. He had to fight, but he did not yield, did not cry, and did not bark. Finally, he got rid from this ill-starred collar and this saved his life. He came to us for help. We took him to Fallbrook hospital. He stayed there for 3 days. In addition, we open our personal hunting for these wild aggressive dogs on our ranch. It was a question of our personal honor. Therefore, we hired one man who promised to get rid of all these wild dogs...

Sometime then Ranger decided that he understand Spanish better and started to spend all his time with our employees. He does not come for food or night sleep even very often. It is very upsetting for us. He goes to everyone who would caress and pet him...

Once, having returned from the next 10-day cruise, I found a very emaciated Ranger in the garden. He lay almost exhausted, tied to a tree

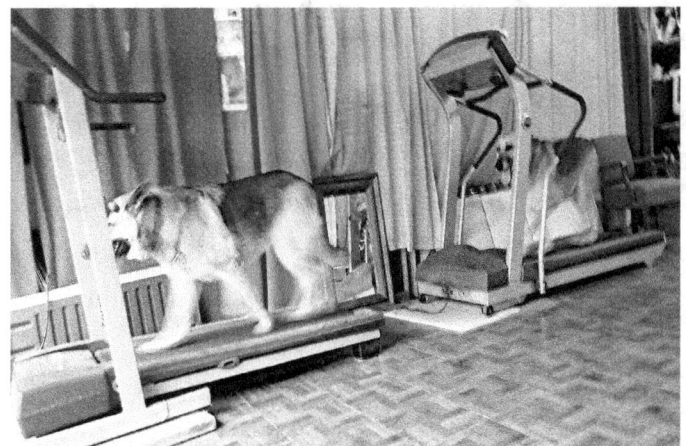

near a bucket of water. Part of his face was in the water, but he did not drink this green, moldy water. I thought that he become strongly infected with microbes, worms and all sorts of parasites, and gave him an antibiotic. After the medication, he felt better, and I took him to the doctor.

There, feeling or smelling something wrong, Ranger came up to me and buried his knees, as if asking for protection. His eyes were almost black from highly dilated pupils. He moved toward me and lightly shoved into my foot. And then he raised his head and in a desperate hopeless rush he whined: Take me out of here

The doctor made X-ray and said that Ranger has cancer. Then he gave him a sleep prick forever.

I am thinking to have another dog - puppy, which I would raise and who would be devoted to our front yard and us.

Memory

When I was about three years old, an orange-brown pooch named Zunka and Tuzik lived in the yard of my grandmother. I remember well how I once stood next to Zunka, to the level with her head, and looked into her big brown eyes. It seemed that this dog really understands all my sorrows. This cute dog was the only living thing in my childhood, which gave me unlimited love and kindness. I also loved her and was not afraid to come close and hug.

However, they were never vaccinated, and soon Tuzik got sick with "rabies" dangerous for people. He barked without stopping and foam was coming out of his mouth. Everyone was very scared, and they said that Zunka probably also got sick. A frowning grandfather took his gun and led both dogs into the woods. He returned later alone. In addition, I never saw them again. It was a tragedy for me. I thought that not everyone whom I loved or whom I was attached to stayed long with me.

In my childhood without motherly love and care, I was so sore for love and kindness that I often remembered this cute little dog with the almost human name Zunka. This bright memory of canine kindness always warmed me in my lonely childhood, and I always loved dogs.

Chow Chow

The Chow Chow, an all-purpose dog of ancient China, presents the picture of a muscular, deep-chested aristocrat with an air of inscrutable timelessness. Dignified, serious-minded, and aloof, the Chow Chow is a breed of unique delights.

Chows are powerful, compactly built dogs standing as high as 20 inches at the shoulder. Their distinctive traits include a lion's-mane ruff around the head and shoulders; a blue-black tongue; deep-set almond eyes that add to a scowling, snobbish expression; and a stiff-legged gait. Chows can have rough or smooth coats of red, black, blue, cinnamon, or cream.

Owners say Chows are the cleanest of dogs: They housebreak easily, have little doggy odor, and are known to be as fastidious as cats. Well-socialized Chows are never fierce or intractable, but always refined and dignified. They are aloof with strangers and eternally loyal to loved ones. Serene and adaptable, with no special exercise needs, Chows happily take to city life.

The Chow Chow, among the world's most singular and possibly oldest breeds, is depicted in artifacts of China's Han Dynasty (c. 206 b.c.), but evidence suggests Chows go back much further and are progenitors of other spitz-type breeds—from the burly Norwegian Elkhound to the dainty Pomeranian.

Chows have played many roles during their long history. At times, they were the lordly companions to Chinese nobles. An emperor of the Tang Dynasty, circa eighth century, was said to have owned a kennel facility that housed some 5,000 Chows and a permanent staff of twice that number. However, over the centuries, they also earned their keep as guarders, haulers, and hunters. Their ancestors were even a food source in the distant past of their densely populated, protein-starved homeland. An ancient breed nickname is the Edible Dog, and a theory behind the origin of the name Chow maintains that it derives from the Cantonese word for "edible."

A more popular explanation of the breed name concerns 18th-century trading ships of the British Empire. At that time, the pidgin-English expression "chow chow" described the small, miscellaneous items within a ship's cargo that were not itemized. "Chow chow" was simply another way of saying "etcetera," and the odd-looking dogs British traders acquired in China were included on the ship's manifest under the catchall "chow chow."

In the 1820s, Chow Chows were exhibited at the London Zoo as the "Wild Dogs of China," but they did not really catch on in the West until Queen Victoria, an inveterate dog lover, acquired one later in the century. Chows were first exhibited in America in the 1890s and were admitted to the AKC in 1903.

Zuynka

One day, sixty years later, in California, I read an advertisement in the local newspaper about selling puppies. I wanted my granddaughter, who lived in the same house with me, to take care of animals too. In our house already lived cat Tosh. In addition, in the yard lived raids rescued dog Ranger. We thought that it would be good for the granddaughter to take a small dog, and went to the nearest settlement to look at the puppies.

In the house of the seller we were met by a variety of small dogs. However, we immediately saw one red and fluffy dog. In addition, on her forehead and neck, she had a white fur, brightly shining among all the rest of her redness. She looked like a ball, fluffy, cheerful and energetic. Therefore, we took her with joy, took her home and began to call Zunka, Zunechka or Zuyu-Zuy. She always stayed near the house, did not run away anywhere, and for a long time was a good company to Ranger. She lived for a long time in our yard without worries. But once she refused to eat and began to swell up much. She was very plump and puffy, not food and did not drink.

A few days later, a veterinarian arrived and gave her a sleep-sting injection. In addition, my husband, Victor, took the dog down and buried her in the middle of the field near the heap.

When we wander through the hills of the ranch, we pass the burial place of Zunka. Then we remember our cheerful friend Ziunku, who lived near the house, was devoted to her booth and the owners, contenting herself with little. Once she barked hysterically loudly, with all her might, but unsuccessfully trying to save our cat Tosh from the teeth of jackals.

Tuzik and Sonia

It is simply impossible to live without dogs on an isolated ranch among hills and citrus plantations. My daughter and granddaughter already lived in different places. My husband and I were left alone and having thought it all over, we decided to take a German Shepherd. We found a dog on the Internet, and drove quite far to get him. We called him Tuzik. Tuzik was also an incredibly intelligent and intuitive dog. We drove him to the dog school, which he graduated from among the best and received a prize.

After the death of the cat Tosha in the teeth of jackals, my husband finally agreed to put a fence on the hill where we lived, i.e. around our house and part of the garden. Tuzik had a lot of energy and when we let him out from behind the fence, he rushed headlong down the hills for hares or other creatures. So once he broke his leg. The operation was unsuccessful, the veterinarian did not observe hygiene, Tuzik received an infection and was sick for a long time. I treated him hard, trying to save his life. He appreciated this, trusted me unconditionally and allowed me to do anything I wanted with him. But he was extremely jealous and did not want to see anyone near us.

Once, Tuzik rushed for a ranch worker who cleaned weeds from the fence of our garden. However, the experienced worker struck our dog on the nose so hard that he came running home with blood. Since then, Tuzik hated all people. He was ready to tear apart any mail carrier approaching our fence.

We hung warning signs everywhere so that no one came to us over the fence. Soon we acquired Sonya the shepherd dog, very cute, cheerful and loving everyone in advance. We were very afraid for the life and health of our most beloved dogs. We tried to give those vitamins and good nutrition. Each dog had its own booth and a huge fenced garden area. In addition, we also bought a simulator for each of them. The dogs knew that they had to run at the gym every day before dinner. When I called them there, they dutifully walked into the garage, jumped onto the cars and ran until I called them back to "eat". They knew a lot of words and listened to me without any frills. But Sonya tried to escape from the exercises, easily jumping off the running machine, and ran to the garden. Then I began to tie her to the machine, until she realized that it was impossible to do this. In general, she

quickly learned that the main thing is to obey and do only what I ordered. Her character was more independent than Tuzik's.

In the summer, they loved to swim in the pool. I threw a toy into the pool for each of them. Tuzik jumped, swam and brought a toy to me. In addition, Sonya reluctantly at first touched the water with her paw, as if feeling if it was very cold. Then she looked at me, checking, suddenly she changed her mind. She did not like water, but she still had to swim for a toy. However, she was tricky here. Sonya returned immediately, instead of reaching the end of the huge pool and exiting there from the other end.

There are many rattlesnakes in California, so all dogs are recommended to attend a special snake recognition lesson. Therefore, we drove Tuzik and Sonya to a ranch where they were taught. It was an incredibly hard lesson for them. A live snake lay on the wasteland, and the instructor led quite close to each dog on a leash. When the dog saw the snake and sensed its smell, the snake hissed, the instructor hit the dog with shock. It was a cruel and panicky lesson for dogs.

But one day my husband was walking Tuzik at nine in the evening, and a rattlesnake bit Tuzik in the leg. He screamed loudly in pain and came running, limping towards me. I immediately gave him vitamin K, which works against poisoning. We jumped into the car and we drove him to the hospital. The animal spent the night there on a drip and, surprisingly to everyone, survived. But after that, something was abnormal with paws and he could not walk on the hot summer ground. He tried to keep in the shade. After that, Tuzik always remembered that if I shouted "no" to him, he immediately stops and looks where the danger comes from.

The animal was a terrific guardian - a guard. He heard all those who drove into our main gate far below the hill, and barked twice a little warning us about it. He had a special bark for different occasions. He also clearly understood and told me with special barking who and where was moving at the ranch. For us, the Tuzik became a doorbell, an alarm system, a main guard and a devoted friend.

He was born as a very talented dog. But his main mission was to protect us. When flirting and adoring Sonya appeared in the courtyard, Tuzik was slightly saddened. In addition, seeing that I take care of Sonya very strongly and do not allow him to growl at her, Tuzik began, over time, to become more attached to my husband. Victor always took Tuzik with him to the truck when he went to check the mailbox.

And Sonya learned from Tuzik everything that he knew and knew how and imitated him. She was incredibly intelligent, emotional, and incredibly impressionable. But her main feature was the love of all around.

German Shepherd

German Shepherd Dogs can stand as high as 26 inches at the shoulder and, when viewed in outline, presents a picture of smooth, graceful curves rather than angles. The natural gait is a free-and-easy trot, but they can turn it up a notch or two and reach great speeds.

There are many reasons why German Shepherds stand in the front rank of canine royalty, but experts say their defining attribute is character: loyalty, courage, confidence, the ability to learn commands for many tasks, and the willingness to put their life on the line in defense of loved ones. German Shepherds will be gentle family pets and steadfast guardians, but, the breed standard says, there is a "certain aloofness that does not lend itself to immediate and indiscriminate friendships."

The German Shepherd Dog (Deutshe Schäferhund) descends from the family of German herding dogs that, until the late 19th century, varied in type from district to district.

In the waning years of the 1800s, a German cavalry officer, Captain Max von Stephanitz, made it his mission to develop the ideal German herder. Von Stephanitz and like-minded breeders crossed various strains from the northern and central districts of Germany, resulting in the ancestors of today's German Shepherd Dog (GSD).

Von Stephanitz co-founded the world's first club devoted to GSDs and spent 35 years promoting and refining the breed. Today, the GSD's versatility is so thoroughly deployed in the performance of myriad tasks that it is easy to forget that the breed was originally created to herd sheep. The GSD's now-famous qualities—intelligence, agility, speed, stealth, and the overall air of firm authority—were forged not in the police academy but in the sheep pasture.

GSDs became popular in the United States in the early 1900s, thanks in part to the adventures of canine movie stars Rin-Tin-Tin and Stronghreart. The GSD is among those German breeds, the Dachshund is another that suffered from anti-German sentiment during and after the world wars. In World War I–era Britain, the breed was referred to as the Alsatian, a name many British dog lovers still prefer.

With the rise of modern livestock management and the decline of herding as a canine occupation, von Stephanitz shrewdly promoted his breed as an ideal K-9 worker. The GSD is today the preferred dog for police and military units the world over.

Interesting Facts

There are about 400 million dogs in the world and there are hundreds of breeds of dogs. The Labrador Retriever is the most popular breed, according to the American Kennel Club. The average dog lives 10 to 14 years. In general, smaller breeds live longer than larger breeds. The fastest breed, the Greyhound, can run up to 44 miles per hour. Perky-eared dogs hear sounds better than floppy-eared dogs.

Puppies love games such as hide and seek. Try that fun game: hide and call your dog's name. Dog will try to find you. Big happy "helicopter" tail wagging is one sign of a really nice dog. Upright, stiff, rapid tail movement is not wagging or "friendly" but indicates a dog who is rather excited and focused.

Puppies grow to half their body weight in the first four to five months. Puppies then take a year or more to gain the other half of their body weight. Puppies can sleep 18 to 20 hours a day during that rapid body growth phase.

Dogs sometimes appear to smile, looks like humans, with an open mouth grinning. This may indicate a relaxed, submissive state. Tired puppies get cranky just like little kids. If you have a fussy puppy, try naptime.

You might want to know several surprising facts about dogs. Your dog is as smart as a 2-year-old toddler.

There is a reason your child and your puppy get along so well. They speak the same language and understand roughly about two hundred fifty words and gestures. Dogs can learn more than 1000 words. Interestingly, dogs and cats both slurp water the same way. Our canine friends bend the tip of their tongue and raise liquid in a column up to their mouths.

Our dog does have a sense of time, and they always miss you when you are gone. In addition, they know when the time for dinner or for a walk. Dogs pick up on our routines and habits. Moreover, they sense well how much time has passed. Your dog's whiskers help him "see" in the dark. Those whiskers pick up on even subtle changes in air currents, providing your pup with information about the size, shape, and speed of things nearby. This allows dogs to better sense approaching dangers or prey, even at night. Dogs only have sweat glands in their paws. It is very important to wet the bottom of their feet on a hot day. Dogs rely on panting to cooling down.

On average, a dog's mouth exerts 320 pounds of pressure. The tests were done on a German shepherd, American pit bull terrier, and Rottweiler. In comparison, human beings exert 120 pounds, white sharks exert 600 pounds, and crocodiles exert a whopping 2,500 pounds. Dogs also have ten more adult teeth than humans do: 42 versus 32. One year-old pup is as physically mature as a 15-year-old human is. Of course, different breeds age a little differently. Large dogs age faster than small ones.

Dog's sense of smell is 1,000 to 10 million times better than ours. Depending on the breed, dogs have between 125 million to 300 million scent glands. However, human has only 5 million. In addition, the part of your dog's brain that controls smell is 40 times larger than yours, even though the size of the canine brain is much smaller than the human. A human's brain is about 1/40th of their body weight while a dog's brain is only 1/125th.

Dogs can hear 4 times as far as humans. Puppies may be born deaf, but they quickly surpass our hearing abilities. Dogs can also hear higher pitched sounds, detecting a frequency range of 67 to 45,000 hertz (cycles per second). The human range is from 64 to 23,000 hertz. In both dogs and humans, the upper end of hearing range decreases with age.

Your dog can smell your feelings. Your pup can pick up on subtle changes in your scent, which can help him figure out how you are feeling.

He smells your perspiration when you become nervous or fearful. This is how dogs can detect certain diseases or know that a household member is pregnant.

All these knowledge and odd facts about dogs gives us a better appreciation of men best friend. They are truly incredible animals and companions.

Scientists about Dogs

"Facial expressions are a key asset in our arsenal of communication methods. Without saying a word, we can alert those around us to our emotional state, ranging from elation to sorrow, simply by flexing a few muscles. Such expressions have evolved to help us connect with one another, avoid danger and work together.

Fellow humans, however, are not the only ones potentially tuning in to the information our expressions convey. According to the results of a study published today in Current Biology, dogs have hacked this silent method of communication, at least enough to distinguish between angry and happy facial expressions.

Dogs and humans share a tight evolutionary bond, which is why veterinarian researchers from the University of Vienna decided to focus on these two species for their study. Dogs are already known to be whizzes at reading us. For instance, they can discriminate between familiar and unfamiliar faces even if just part of the face is shown in a photograph. Whether they actually recognize emotions, however, had not been conclusively investigated before.

The Vienna researchers needed to design an airtight experimental setup, free from potential emotional proxies that the canines could use to cheat the test. Dogs might learn, for example, that the presence of teeth corresponds with happy expressions but then wrongly interpret the flash of pearly whites in a snarl or shout.

To bypass any confounding variables, the researchers trained about a dozen pet dogs to distinguish between a neutral, forward-looking face and the back of the same person's head, using a touch screen that the dogs operated with their nose. If they chose the forward-facing image correctly, they received a small reward.

After training the dogs with one familiar face, the researchers found that their subjects had little difficulty applying what they learned—the universal signs of human happiness or anger—to photos of faces they had never seen before. The team noted, however, that dogs were slower to select correctly the angry faces, perhaps a sign that the canines could already associate mad-looking expressions with bad outcomes and thus wanted to avoid those faces.

As far as the authors know, this is the first time researchers have shown that one animal species can recognize the emotional state of another (humans recognizing emotions in animals doesn't count). The team points out, though, that it would come as no surprise if other animals have similar powers of interspecies communication, since the information offered by facial expressions could be handy for survival. A lioness recognizing whether a wildebeest is preparing to angrily charge or to flee just by regarding the squint of its eyes and flare of its nostrils could mean the difference between a mortal injury and dinner.

Before the authors delve into the greater animal kingdom, though, they plan to further explore their canine findings. Experiments with puppies could lend insight into whether facial expression recognition is something dogs learn over their lives or if it is something more innate. And trials with wolves could indicate whether human breeders bestowed emotion recognition in their canine companions via artificial selection, or whether that trait was something dogs' ancient relatives developed on their own simply by living in the vicinity of humans.

While the initial controlled laboratory findings do not prove that, your dog is watching your every facial move for clues about how you are feeling, they do open up the possibility that dogs are even more empathetic best friends than we thought.

***

Love your dog

Intellectually dogs are at the level of two-year-old children. They understand up to 250 words and gestures, count up to five, and can solve simplest mathematical problems.

In Russia, dogs were able to adapt the metro to their own needs. In search of food, they learned to travel by public transport through the most populated areas.

Dogs do not like hugs. For them, it is a sign of dominance. So, stop finally doing it.

Dogs distinguish ultrasonic whistle. Knowing this, Paul McCartney recorded this sound at the end of the song "Day of Life" purposefully for his Scottish Shepherd.

In ancient China, the emperor's last line of defense was a small Pekingese breed dog. She hid herself in the sleeve, but jumped out and threw herself at the enemy in the case of a danger.

Lord Byron learned that the Cambridge did not allow his dog to be in the Trinity College where he studied. Then, he brought a bear cub instead.

Wet nose dog needed to determine the direction of the smell.

In the ancient Greece, they invented the spiked collars to protect dogs' necks from being attacked by wolves.

If your dog smells like chips, it does not mean that she ate your nest egg, do not rush to scold her. There is such a phenomenon "Frito Feet", and it is due to the accumulation of bacteria on their paws. This is why dog can smell like corn chips. You have to compliance with the rules of hygiene after a walk and wash dog's paws.

***

A dog boxer "Banks" and Goose "Button" became friends after the dog had an accident and was blind. Gus helped him to his feet, becoming his guide. "Button" helps the dog by his neck, directs him by shouts, and never leaves him alone.

In fact, dogs drink, folding the tongue in a shape of a spoon, but not up, but down - from the palate.

Puppies have 28 teeth, and adult dogs - 42.

The heart of a large dog, like the heart of a human, it beats from 60 to 100 beats per minute in a calm state. In the small dogs, it beats 100-140.

72% of dog owners believe their wards can predict a storm. An excellent hearing helps them to predict the weather 10 times better than a person.

There are three eyelid pairs in dogs: the upper, lower, and blinking membranes, which lubricate and protect the eye.

Dogs have 1,700 taste buds. For comparison, a person has 9,000.

A dog smells 10,000–100,000 times better than a human does. Keep your goodies in a safe place.

Speaking of goodies, chocolate is dangerous for dogs. It contains theobromine, which affects the central nervous system and the heart muscle of the dog. In humans, this substance breaks down enzymes.

Remember, according to the dog, you are the leader of the pack. At least it should be.

Dogs instinctively require the approval of the leader before any act.

Dogs, like people, may hiccup when they eat or drink too fast.

Like human children, Chihuahuas are born with a soft spot (the fontanel) in the upper part of the skull, which hardens with age.

"They always come out dry" - these words can be fully attributed to Newfoundland dogs that do not get wet in the water, and, thanks to their webbed feet, are excellent swimmers.

The fastest dog is a Greyhound named "Star Title". Its maximum speed is 67.32 km / h, and this record has not been broken since 1994.

Obesity is problem number one in the health of dogs.

In total, there are 703 breeds of purebred dogs.

45% of dogs sleep in the master's bed.

Dogs judge objects first by their movement, then by their brightness and, finally, by their form.

"Rin Tin Tin" was the first dog to be a "Hollywood star," and, like all celebrities. He himself signed all of his 22 film contracts by a sign of his paw.

The longer the dog's nose, the more effective its internal cooling system.

In 1988, at the customs in the United States, dogs "Rocky" and "Barco" were patrolling the border (known as "Cocaine Avenue") between Texas and Mexico very well. The Mexican drug barons promised $30,000 reward for their heads.

The Boxer dogs got that name because of their manner of playing with their front paws.

Chihuahua dogs are named after the state of Chihuahua in Mexico, where they were discovered.

Only after the 1st month do puppies start to see normally.

"Lundehund" dogs have six fingers on each paw.

Dogs are mentioned 14 times in the Bible.

Dogs have learned to drive a car. The New Zealand Society "Protection of Animal Rights" set up an experiment, as a result of which three dogs learned to drive a car in a straight line and even turn around.

The highest dog breed is Great Dane.

During the crash of Titanic, three dogs survived Newfoundland, Pomeranian, and Pekingese. Of course, they were with the passengers of the first class.

The South Korean scientist Hwan Usok cloned dog for the first time in 2005. Today this procedure costs $ 100,000.

The oldest dog, a terrier "Max", turned 30 years old in August 2013. By a human standard, it would be 210 years old!

If a dog's tail wagging to the left (relative to the quadruped), it means as a signal "Attention, anxiety".

The highest dog is the German "Great Dane". When he is standing up on his paws, his height is two, 20 meters.

The smallest dog is a Chihuahua named "Heaven Sent Brandy". Her weight is 900 grams. She is as tall as a can of Coca-Cola.

The first animal rights law was adopted in Japan in the 17th and 18th centuries. According to it, the killing of dogs was punishable by execution. The townspeople should have addressed the stray dogs as "highly honored

51

Dog."

"Canary Islands" named after epy dogs (from the Latin "canis"), because the locals idolized these dogs. The canary bird also named after these islands.

According to the 14th century statute book "Metropolitan Justice", in Ancient Russia, the dog was valued as one ox, three horses or a flock of sheep.

Belka and Strelka

Dogs are direct descendants of wolves.

The dog owners move %66 more than other people.

The predatory nature of the dog determines its nutrition. It must be as biologically appropriate as possible. It should be the same as the wolves have: more animal protein, less carbohydrates.

In Russia people call "@" sign a "dog". However, in other countries, it is a snail, a monkey, a strudel (in Hebrew), a herring marinated (in Czech and Slovak) and a moon ear (in Kazakh).

Belka (Белка, literally, "Squirrel" or alternatively "Whitey") and Strelka (Стрелка, "Little Arrow") spent a day in space aboard Korabl-Sputnik 2 (Sputnik 5) on 19 August 1960 before safely returning to Earth.

Laika (Russian: Лайка; c. 1954 – 3 November 1957) was a Soviet space dog who became one of the first animals in space, and the first animal to orbit the Earth. When in the USSR the dog Laika was sent into space, it was obviously known that she would die.

Today

Today is January 7. We always celebrated this special day in our homeland with our close friends and loved ones around our festival table and gifts. Today it was good to walk around the ranch on the wet ground and breathe the fresh air after last night's rain. Happiness is when there is no dust around. We picked several of the remaining persimmons from the trees.

Dogs are always waiting for us near the door to come out and do something together instead of just sitting in front of the TV. I took them around the house to smell huge amount of narcissus and others, similar to them. I picked some flowers, put them in a vase, and that sweet smell filled the house. These precious moments the dogs shared with me. This day will never happen again. What did you do to make it enjoyable for some who are near you and for yourself? – Peace and happiness are around you for a special one to see and enjoy...

The attitude of a man towards the animals is an indicator of his soul. Unfortunately, not many people remember that their pets also have feelings and simple thoughts. Our faithful pets closely watch your every step, trying to please you with their love and devotion. Their inner goal is to serve the master and make him happy.

As long as I can remember, we always had dogs and cats in our house or in the yard. They were my best friends. I watched them, played and ran with them. When my dogs or cats were sick, I learned how to be their doctor. Our lives were bonded tightly and I was living through their happy young time, and was companionate for their old age and some tragedies.

Afterword

Cats and dogs understand everything around them, and have their own world, consisting in serving you. They feel deeply, love you with no conditions, and are infinitely devoted to you. They could tell many funny or sad stories about their lives, if you want to listen to them.

We always need to remember that when we tame animals, we are forever responsible for them. Do not give up, do not leave them to the mercy of fate under any circumstances. Even when you are fleeing the war zone, protect them and keep all family members together. Your loving cats and dogs will always be your joy in any conditions and sorrows.

Our Favorite Pets

The cat and dog have long been the most popular pets. They are the most intelligent, easily trained and the most comfortable to live at home. In a cat people often, see a reflection of the feminine features. And a dog is mostly a symbol and expression of male characteristics. Of course, it all depends on the size of a dog, its breed and who brings him up. Traditionally, the dog lived in a yard, acting as a watchdog. And the cat often lived in a house, creating more comfort and coziness.

As we noted, over time a cat and a dog adopt the features of their owners and became alike. However, it always depends on how much time the hosts spend with their pets, how attentive they are to the pets' needs. Moreover, animals are boundlessly devoted not only to the house, but they become attached to the master and love him wholeheartedly. They are always trying to please us as much as they can. Most importantly, they do not know the word "betrayal."

However, sometimes we see that people get a cat or a dog for their children mostly for an amusement. When the animals are small, people enjoy them as living toys. However, not many people think in advance how things will be when the pets grow up. Then, having played enough with a puppy or kitten, without having taught them good manners, people might heartlessly throw pets to the mercy of fate, without thinking about the suffering of the animal.

In good families, pets become family members, and adults teach their children to understand that their pets have their own feelings and simple thoughts. Parents emphasize how important it is to care for the pets, to communicate with and love them, as people should love each other. It is pet care that brings up the best qualities in a person. And it is the best to start doing this from childhood.

Later on, it is clear that the attitude towards animals is a person's character. We treat animals in the same way as we relate to other people:

as attentively, with love and care, as our soul lets us or we are able to. How much time and effort a person gives to a cat or dog, in the same way he would act in the human relationship. Attention and treatments of animals is like a litmus test of human characteristics.

    The old wisdom said: treat your pets in a way as you want to be treated.

About Author

Elena originally is from an old aristocratic Russian/Greek family. She graduated from the prestigious Leningrad State University as a philologist-linguist, and holds a Master Degree (Slavonic Philologist, Linguist, and Journalist). She has more than 40 years of job experience in different areas of art education, literature, music, dance and theater. She worked as an assistant producer in Russian cinematography, sound assistant of movie productions, Radio journalist, and newspaper correspondent. Then, she owned her own businesses and traveled the world.

In 1996, Elena met a wonderful American gentleman, a Dr. PhD, a businessman, Victor Pankey, got married and moved to the USA. While living in California, her main hobbies are writing, traveling, teaching, performing and dancing.

While living in California, she writes fun books and teaches dancing. Elena developed a tango course, which has helped people improve the quality of their lives and marriages. She is the author of several fun books about Argentine Tango dancing, art, animals and adventures. More: www.TangoCaminito.com

Copy Rights Page

Author - Elena Pankey. All rights reserved. No part of this publication may be reproduced, distributed, or transmitted in any form or by any means, including photocopying, recording, or other electronic or mechanical methods, without the prior written permission of the publisher, except in the case of brief quotations embodied in critical reviews and certain other noncommercial uses permitted by copyright law. For permission requests, write to the publisher, addressed "Attention: Permissions Coordinator," at the address below.

The title of a book was printed in the United States of America. ISBN-13: 978-1-950311-38-5. The main category of the book – Pets. Other category – Family. First Edition, 2019. Photos by Elena Pankey.

Get a new book: www.TangoCaminito.com

www.ingramcontent.com/pod-product-compliance
Lightning Source LLC
Chambersburg PA
CBHW052208110526
44591CB00012B/2131